Anybody
Everybody

Anybody
Everybody

Anybody, Everybody
beautiful plain
soft   hard
lovable   ordinary
not quite normal

people who scream and kiss
faces closed tight or open
yellow and black
and white
people wearing masks
armed with words
shy, lame, or with wings
women and men
kings, slaves, exiles.

all who hunger
        love
        live
now you read this

you have never seen
everyone the whole world over
everyone there is

No one at any time
has seen them.

Written on a wall
in the city where I live
are these words:
people die, people do not find happiness.

People kill people, reduce them to poverty, slavery,
make them frightened, speechless. The strong abuse the weak.
Those with power desire still more. And with one stroke
they kill the water, the air, the earth, hope.

10

Why do people do that?
I asked my father, when I was still small.

Not everyone does that, he said.

It was a Sunday evening in September
I was seven years old
the whole world was at war.
A man walked down our deserted street
yelling, selling newspapers
I shivered with dread when I heard him.

A week later I heard that voice again
I hid away under my parent's bed.
My father lifted me up,
put on my little coat,
and bought a newspaper.
He said, you must never be afraid of people.
The newspaper man was small and shy.

From that time on I have tried
not to fear people.

From that time on
I have also seen their fear—
the frightened hand that strikes
the tongue that lies.
The soldier who must kill
is also a frightened child.

It was in those days too
that my father told me about God.
He said, the city where we live
is a city without peace.
But there will come a city
filled with peace
and it will cover the whole world.

Our home was a safe home.
The world was threatening
for there was war.
But danger cannot touch us here, I thought,
for we belong together.

My father said,
there shall be no more rich and poor
no kings, no slaves,
no more hunger, no more aggression,
but light enough and bread for everyone.
That is God's dream, what God wills.
I shivered, this time from happiness.
And each time I heard these words
it was the same.
My father said,
that city people build by doing good.
God is the still small voice within
that speaks to you
and tells you what is good
in a voice that you can understand,
so that you also know how to do right
for the one who is beside you.

That voice speaks in you.

You may call him mother,
father, love, heart of light.
When you pray to him
use these words:

Our father who is in a secret place
may your name be known and carried through
may your kingdom of peace be established
may your will be done: heaven on earth
give us today our bread, and tomorrow,
and forgive us our trespasses
as we forgive those who trespass against us
and do not try us beyond what we can bear
and deliver us from the power of the unjust.

What is praying? I asked.
It is listening to the voice·
it is longing for that city to rise up
longing to see it
even in your life, my father said.

But as I grew
wherever I looked
whatever I saw
no city of peace—

here and there perhaps a house
two or three people
who do not bite and devour each other.

And these words
about that kingdom of God
which when I was small
I had heard earnestly
grew vague and dim before my eyes.

The older the more clearly
I saw them going, people
travelling long roads to nothing.

Most of them had a god
and many spoke of him
and they all prayed
for money or for health or to be rid of fear
but apparently
this did not make them happy.

They were young
they grew old.

18

They died.

And no god intervened
and there was no peace.

My father was no longer young
(though not old either)
when he died suddenly.

At his funeral
a song was sung
about everything—so it seemed—
that I had seen and always thought
in my life, up to that day.
I heard them singing:

"As for man his days are as grass
as a flower of the field so he flourisheth
for the wind passeth over it and it is gone
and the place thereof shall remember it no more."

This is the final word
all there is to know
I thought.
There is nothing more to sing
after this song.

Then it continued
and I heard:

"But the love of God shall endure
for all who accept his word
and carry it out."

21

In the silence which followed
I recalled the old words
which I had once heard earnestly
and had remembered
but not understood.

"May your name be known and carried through
May your kingdom of peace be established."

And I knew with certainty
that I would never again be free of these words
("the love of God shall endure")

Returning home I searched in the book
he so often used to read
for the words I had heard sung.
They were not hard to find
on much-fingered pages
somewhere in the middle
of that book called the Bible.

On the flyleaf he had written:
"This is the book of the poor.
If you want to understand it
you must go and be on their side.
They are almost anybody, everybody."

I read as if my life depended on it.
Some passages
he had underlined in red.

"I begin my complaint against you:
you who tread down the weak, the innocent,
and maltreat those who are not guilty.
Do what is just, seek righteousness.
Let righteousness stream like a fountain,
and justice like streams of living water.
You who prepare your murderous attacks against the poor,
it is because of you that the world topples."

Reading this I heard a voice speak in myself
and what my eyes read
that voice spoke within me.

"Hear O Israel:
Love the stranger who is here beside you
for you were once a stranger also
and a slave in a foreign land."

And when I looked up from the book
and looked at the world around me   _
I realized
that what I had read
was the truth,
what really happened,
was indeed the life
of most people of the world.

What must I think?
Where should I begin?

And it was as if I stood
alone
against world powers.

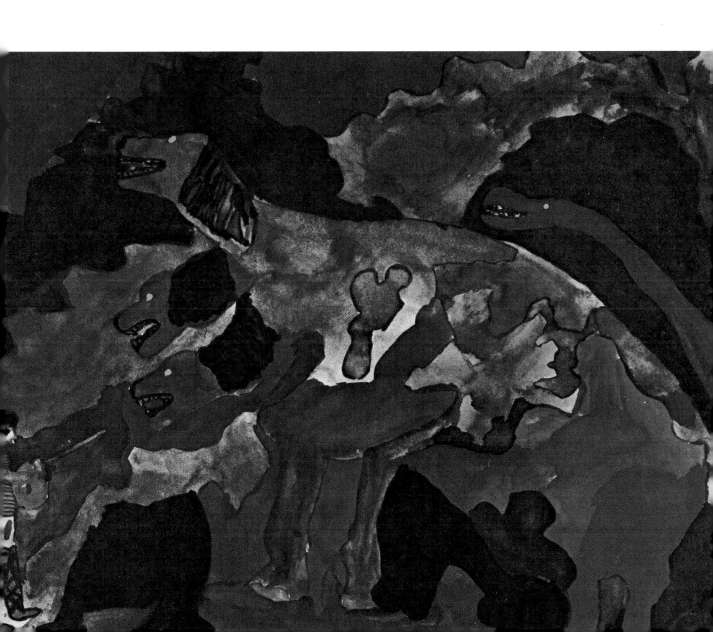

I had friends. I told them
what had come over me.
They said, "Will you never learn to accept
that the world is as it is?
You are a dreamer;
you cannot reconcile yourself to facts."

There were other facts I gradually learned to see,
another world—though still in bud-like form,
yet just as real as hunger, enmity—
budding in people.

I saw people doing what they had to do:
bearing their children, burying their dead
and fighting for the stranger there beside them
for bread and clothing
for work and housing
and the right to speak.

I found also
people—beautiful plain
          women   men
          lame   with wings
          living together
as if that kingdom of peace was already begun
and none of them in need or suffering.

One night I dreamed
that I was sailing on an open sea
in a boat small as a nutshell
beneath dark clouds, and it stormed.
Then walking towards me a light across the water,
and in that light three people carrying staffs
who called out: do not fear.
There were oars for me to row with.

The four of us rowed together to the shore
and then they disappeared
into the dawning of a new day.

All these things happened to me
long before you were born,
you who now read this.
No one had even imagined your existence
but it is for you that I have written down these things
for perhaps through what is written here
you will find your way to the book of the poor
and go and stand at their side.

When you were little you drew people,
and you drew good people.
If you look carefully you will see
that people can be good.
They can hear and they can think,
they can learn and they can grow,
they can go, turn around again, or go on further.

You must not be afraid of people.
Also, you do not stand alone
against world powers.
You must know that.
Everywhere there are people
who do what is right

people who resist death and injustice
who are building the city of peace.
If you look carefully
you will see people going
towards another world
and where people are going
there is a road
you can go with them.

Person after person,
two, three, three thousand,
never to be numbered
a great procession through the ages.

Number them if you can.

Number the grains of sand
on the shores of the sea
or the stars in the sky.

One, more than all of them, one of us
was the spokesman of God's vision
of that for which everything was first begun.
"May your kingdom of peace be established."

What God always longed for
it was he
and it has been seen.

Who spoke like him?
Because of his words
many understood the meaning of their lives.
And a force streamed out of him
which built peace and healed
and still does.

The time is ripe
God's kingdom draws close by
change your way of life.

Happy you who are poor
for God's kingdom belongs to you.
Happy you who now weep
for you shall rejoice.

Watch carefully that your spirit
is not trampled under
by the troubles of this life.
Be watchful and pray.

Whoever holds on to his life
shall lose it.
Whoever gives his life
shall find it.

I say to you:
Love your enemies.

Messenger of God's will
head of our procession.

Jesus of Nazareth
leader and sharer

Jesus Messiah.

There are places
in this world
where he is recognized
and known.

Churches, here and there
a house.

Two or three people
in hidden places.

Places where they
pray, believe
in the coming
of another world.
Where there will be
bread offered for all
where there will be
life enough for all

that kingdom of peace
all for everybody.

And where the faces of the poor
are seen.
Those who have nothing
of this all
no share in life
no right to speak.

They are
almost anybody, everybody.

Not because blind fate
rules this universe,
not because the world is poor
and nature vicious,
but because the strongest rule
and the strong kill the weak,
and those with money and power
desire still more—
that is why the world topples.

You who live in this godforgotten world
do not forget who you are yourself:
a drop of water, a seed on the wind
flowers in the open field—
sharer of all.

But also remember his name—
"God of the poor"—
and remember the son of man
who was the spokesman for that God.

And seek a place
where people speak and live
in his spirit.

And learn to understand
that voice which speaks
to you from far off
and within to tell you
what is good.

So that you choose
to stand on the side
of the poor and to walk
down their road.

37

Here, for that long journey
is one word more from him
it may perhaps comfort you.

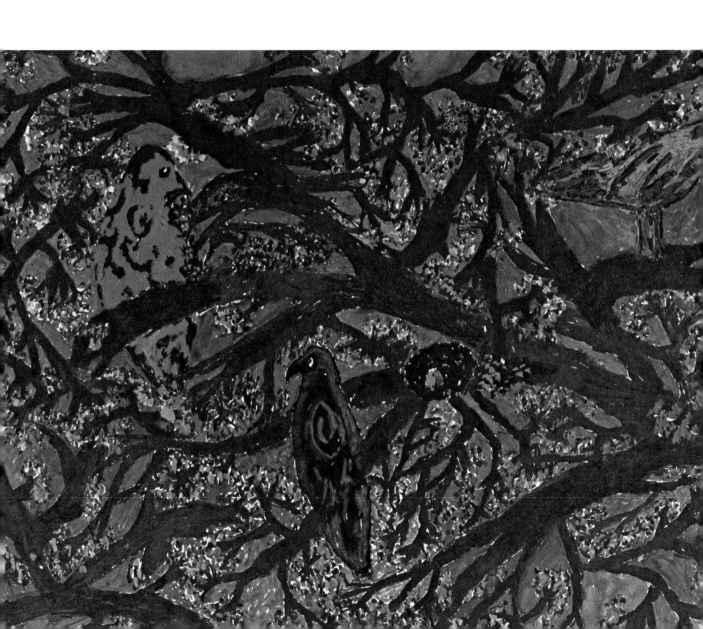

Do not be anxious for your life,
for food and drink,
for your body or clothing.
Life is more than food and drink,
your body is more precious than clothing.

And the flowers of the wayside
who neither spin nor weave
but simply blossom?
Solomon in all his glory
was not as beautiful as one of them.

Flowers which blossom today
and tomorrow are no more,
but your father who is in heaven
clothes them and cares for them.
How could he then not care for us?

Seek his kingdom, and do justice
and he will provide for you.

Sometimes it will seem
as if you walk with wings.

Like people who are journeying
towards a new beginning.

And you will see, in your life too,
a glimpse, a tiny spark
from his kingdom of peace—
people at peace.

At times you will know
as surely as your own existence
that the love of God will endure.

And who he will be
in a new heaven
on a new earth
when death shall be no more:

God in people.

God in people

So far no one
has seen him
but he shall be God
new and for all time.

All in all.

COLOPHON

© World Council of Churches, 150, rte de Ferney, 1211 Geneva 20,
Switzerland, 1981
Translated from Dutch by Wendy Shaffer
Original Dutch title: *Alle mensen van de wereld*
Layout: Matthieu Vroemen, Maastricht, The Netherlands
Lithos: Crouzen B.V., Maastricht, The Netherlands
Printed in Switzerland by Imprimerie Corbaz, Montreux

ISBN: 2-8254-0658-9

This book was originated by the World Council of Churches to mark
the International Year of the Child. It is an attempt to bring
the worldwide oikoumene closer to the life of the congregation.
The illustrations were chosen from a collection of more than
a thousand drawings which the World Council received from
children in all parts of the world, especially the Federal
Republic of Germany, Great Britain, Haiti, India, Italy, Latin
America, the Netherlands, and Sri Lanka.

Huub Oosterhuis is a Roman Catholic priest living in Amsterdam,
where he leads an ecumenical student "ekklesia" and cultural
centre. He is one of the most popular modern Dutch hymn-writers
and has written a number of best selling books, among them his
famous collection of contemporary prayers *Your Word is Near* and
The Children of the Poor Man, published in the RISK book series of the
World Council of Churches in 1980.